D0865268

PORCH WATCH

Ansie Baird

Advance praise for Porch Watch

Ansie Baird's new book is a lovely mix of wit, emotional range, and craft--a craft that responds to each of its poetic occasions in a voice that has been tutored through her earlier collections to be sharp, humorous, intelligent, able to be at once acerbic and honestly emotional. *Porch Watch*--with its implication of constant vigil--is full of warm appreciations of friends, of elegies that compose the broken heart into a right ritual of mourning: into, indeed, a style of blessing, each one scattered where she wants all her friends ashes to be scattered "in the fields of praise." I love the jaunty fortitude of these poems, each one demonstrating (without a trace of self pity or self indulgence) how a rendered life, shadows and all, can be taken on, fully engaged with. "True things," she says, "make up the miracles of your life." Her poems are just such big-hearted, open-eyed true things.

-*Eamon Grennan*

Elegance is only one of the many words that come to mind when reading Ansie Baird's new poems *Porch Watch*, though heartbreaking is most certainly another. The elegies to poets like John Logan and Hayden Carruth and to her sister are good examples, but the heart of this book are the poems to herself. In "Kitchen Wisdom" she tells her grandson, when he asks if she fears death, "No, not scared, exactly", that what she fears is missing the world and watching him grow up. A remarkable accounting can be found in these brave and honest poems, all the more reason to relish their elegance. In a poem about her house, she manages to also describe her life: "This is a house composed / of paper and stucco and oak,/ a house held together by / sloping doors and hope/ by climbing vines and desire adorning the supporting walls." Yes, hope and desire, and love, there's plenty of all that to be found in these beautiful and moving poems. Indeed.

-*Philip Schultz*

Ansie Baird's easy intimacy opens the doors of these poems and invites us into her confidence. *Porch Watch* looks at a life, or maybe a collection of lives — the wheres and hows and might-have-beens of memory. In a style that shimmers off the page, Baird writes of loss, living, hosting, and having. These poems are nothing short of spectacular.

-*Janet McNally*

Reader: meet this self. This self of non-obvious, hard-won, elegant wisdom. This self who follows up on her lines' implications, to tender tough talk. Who neither redeems disappointment, nor dissembles the satisfaction of aestheticizing it into something usable. This self invites us to lie seemingly right in the soil of her mind's landscape, till we note patterns in primary thought glancing off reflection, before the two coalesce in artful indistinction. A mild vertigo as memory mediates presentness, as the self queries and delights in her words on the page, as "I" is suddenly slyly styled as "she." This self has earned the hubris to alter Lear, her unabashed rhymes, and echoes of echoes of loved poems and songs, yet writes, too, what the inner ear might mishear, or chance to ride: was that "endearing" or "enduring" – or both and more? This self slings tone to attune the matter-of-fact to its rhetoricity, this self knows reckoning to face the worst (as never worst). Small and larger disappointment vies with Death, the latter perhaps the sweeter consort in many-pitched elegies doing all we can ask of friend or lover: make us live again. Here is Mother's despair and labor, Father as keeper of language and evened love. Reader: witness this self knowing itself – a self assured by its self-honesty – its considered exposure to emotional risk. And see it re-gather into a loved self. That is not consolation. It's pleasure.

-*Judith Goldman*

Foundlings Press
Buffalo, NY
www.FoundlingsPress.com

Author photo copyright (c) 2019 by Mark Dellas
Cover art copyright (c) 2019 by Whiting Tennis

Printed in the United States of America

First Edition, 2019

ISBN: 978-0-9997539-4-1

Porch Watch

~~Ansie Baird~~

Ansie Baird

FOUNDLINGS

*For Mary + Jim —
at our 60th VC
reunion.
Salve!
(till
next
time)*

6/19

Ansie

Dedicated to

THEO
JAKE
OLIVER
ALEXANDER
ABIGAIL
CHARLOTTE
DANIEL
EVA
NAT
SAM

CONTENTS

… if ever called upon
    to favor Nature,
    I'll take the aspens.
    They tremble in an appropriate way.
    They know what's coming.

TRANSLATIONS

For she mastered the art of leaving, my mother.
Long ago in a hotel room she began,
Brittle limbs of winter cracking at the window,
Which melted into tears, into flames
Consuming her, a real cigarette
Abandoned on the floor. The match had done
What it was designed to do. It burned.
If I were to tell you I stood robed in white
Like an angel, white gauze mask
Above my mouth, white cap, white
Paper slippers over my shoes,
If I were to say I stood that way
Beside her bed the night she died
And sang to her "The Marseillaise" so
She could remember France and childhood,
You would not believe me.

For he mastered the art of leaving, my father.
Like an aloof statue, perhaps Moses, he sat
Propped in his armchair, his exile.
Five years his face froze above silence,
His one good hand clenched in a fist of fury.
Kill me! it said. Speak to me! I wanted to shout.
I let him down every day for five years.
He was going away all along, taking the entire
Luxurious English language
Tucked in a satchel under his one good arm.
I fled the city whenever I could.
The day he died I was asleep
On an island in another country
Where I could not speak the language.
A stranger translated his death at the front desk.
He made me understand.

LANDSCAPE

Alive, lively
all sorts of
strange creatures
stay here and
sprout. Useful
things like
wild flowers
and berries.

So many names
I do not remember.
Woodbine.

Something in my
brain went little
so I've lost
my words. Per-
plexing, for
instance.
Winter days
go different.
What. And how.
And also.

Useful things
are growing
in my yard.
I cannot tell you why.

EARLY VERSION OF HAMLET

On a tiny swing at the top of the massive castle
a man dressed as a jester in tights blazing with stars
is doing cartwheels while blowing bubbles which
glitter in the guttering light from dozens of candles
as a maiden clad in gauzy fabric slithers from behind
an embroidered arras in the hallway but it's too late.

When he reaches the parapet, not one rough guard
recognizes him because time has changed everything
including his accent, his gestures, even the robes
he wears in a foreign fashion. When he speaks
commandingly, they rush towards him, swords
at the ready. A stranger will intervene.

Each origami bird, folded in precise shape, flies
right, taking the air, heading straight for first light,
a slit window at the head of the curving stair, not
a hiding place. Paper art has no place here
in this austere expanse of stone and loneliness, heated
by wrath and open hearths lit with the ash of lost fathers.

Week after day after moment, Hamlet knows not seems.

WHAT I REMEMBER
FROM DIVORCE COURT

I'm pretty sure they all stood up
when the judge entered.
That might not be accurate.
I was pretty sure to have been
in some kind of a daze.
There was not much notable
about the room, more like
an abandoned hallway with some
doorways strung along the sides.
But I could be wrong.
It might have been solid
oak with polished brass trim
and blue velvet wall-hangings.
I've recently discovered
nothing is impossible.

I kept my eyes on the corner
of the ceiling so as not to cry.
My lawyer was elderly and kind.
The other lawyer was handsomer
but he looked like a dapper idiot.
His hair was damp, as though he'd
just come off the squash court.
Perhaps with the absent partner.
Maybe I just made that up.
The dapper man left the room
while the judge asked why it was
I wanted a divorce.

Wanted? Not precisely
the word I'd have chosen.

But things go around and
things go around
and it came down
to this particular place
on this particular day.
So I told my graphic side of the story
and it was over in maybe fifteen minutes.
Divorce granted. Gavel slammed.
The kind lawyer walked me to the elevator.
Well, he asked, How do you feel now?
I can't remember where I parked my car.

INTRODUCTION, AT LAST

At the intermission at Symphony Hall,
they finally met. She thought that all
the weeks and years of their estrangement
must be resolved. So, by arrangement,
he and the woman climbed the stair.
She kept her calm and waited there.
The three of them were civilized,
the proper tone, she recognized,
for chat. It was mercifully brief
and later she felt a keen relief
combined with sadness. What the hell.
The trio parted, saved by the bell.

She altered for her use a line
from "Lear" that fit the ending fine:
My Lord, pray you, undo this buckle.
And, faintly, she could hear God chuckle.

MOVING FURNITURE

I ask you to help me move
a heavy table at a family party.
You're my former husband, here
with your long-term attachment.
I say: *Oh, hi! Could you*
just give me a hand with this
trestle table? I can't move it alone.
And you do, you give me a hand.

You're thinner than when we last
embraced, some twelve years ago,
a desperate summer. Okay,
thinner isn't so bad. Or balder.
You used to have lavish
blond curls I longed to grab
and run my hands through.
But you weren't that type. So
I stroked them from a distance.

Now it's Christmas Eve. We stand
at opposite ends of an immovable
table and you look old but endearing,
also enduring. Familiar and strange,
as I must, also. Together, we lean our
fragile weight into something solid
we each could have managed alone
when we were young and careless,
decades ago.

THE CLAMOR OF FATHERS

I'm out of syllables
she said and
what is worse
my father prowls
the neighborhood
scattering verbs
like bird seed
quick   quick
clatters ash cans
pick   pick
pacing the alley
hop   skip
lugging language
in his sack
doubles back
click   clack
cane taps tops
of iron railings
climbing up
stick at my neck

not for long
Old Man
don't forget
you're supposed
to be dead
back off or
I'll bash you to
silence, she said

EVEN FRAGMENTS

His lavish phrases
urged her to attempt
climbing concrete stairs
when every elevator failed.
She was easily persuaded
by his letter saying:
Come now. I am gilded with expectation.

A woman bending toward blooms
after long arid afternoons,
a woman who has known ardor
in the bones of her throat,
needs little persuasion.
She cherished that phrase:
Come. Now. I am gilded with expectation.

It was he who praised
the honey-colored ramparts
of her hair, he who woke her
at morning, his whistling
in the kitchen a simple seduction
so far from town, scent of toast
beneath the frozen eaves.

A kind of rushing is all she recalls
from their forgotten language.
Even fragments
keep her from grieving,
each fragment some sort of
consolation, a clump
of juniper stuck on her tongue.

DOOR BELL

If it couldn't be you
it must be the King
It couldn't be you
because you're tangled
in thickets and brambles
and ditches one after
another or clutched
in the tops of trees
it cannot be true
it couldn't be you
whose big heart
checked out
after too many years
to count
if truth be told
you weren't even old
unless some damn fool
declares seventy five
is plenty of being alive

Not me I counted
on you to keep
climbing the stair
to my tower forever
no time to spare
at least eleven more
years you'd be there

Now when footsteps
sound in the hall
coming near
I kid myself
perhaps he is here
but then when I hear
brisk knocks on the door
not the way I used to before
I know in my heart it
couldn't be you so
when I hear the bell ring
it must be the King.

DREAMSCAPE

George VI lay sprawled across my lap.
I said, I've never held the hand of a king
Before. He said, It's just like any other hand,
An ordinary hand. And so it was.
I ran my hand over his tweed-clad leg.
So soft, I said, I've never felt such tweed.
Cashmere, he murmured, reaching for my face.
We managed to elude the waiting crowd,
He in a wide-brimmed homburg, I cloaked
In my usual aplomb as we strode
The wide-brimmed avenue seeking solitude.
Nothing untoward took place. He looked rather
Frail, I was solicitous. Both of us knew
It couldn't last. We cherished the day.

THE ROMANOVS AND I

I was quite sure I was going to marry
Michael Romanov after I met him in Paris
in 1949. I was twelve and we lived in
shabby dwellings for a year, my father
on sabbatical from teaching and my
mother reacquainting herself with all
her childhood friends and relatives
after a hiatus of sixteen years.

My father seemed to know everyone
and one of his dearest friends
turned out to be Irina Romanov,
grandneice of the last czar.
Her family fled to France before the
Revolution, where they lived a
luxurious life while we visitors
caught tiny glimpses of their past.

Michael may have been — oh, twenty
or twenty-two or -three when we met.
His manners were impeccable but
not artificial. No hand kissing and
that nonsense. Just pure charm as
well as staggering good looks.
I was riveted.

One afternoon we went there to tea,
served by a young woman in a
scalloped white lace apron. She
curtsied when introduced to us,
which seemed appropriate to me

because I'd always been taught to
curtsy when introduced to my elders.

We had scones and jam along with
puff pastries with caramelized sugar
spun into fanciful decorations on top.
Michael and I talked and talked.
I was seldom at a loss for words,
even when dazzled.

Anyway, I was positive he was as
enchanted by me as I by him, I in
my blue serge skirt and prim white
blouse, he in soft tweeds and
a silk necktie in pastels. Perhaps
he was this nice to everyone. How
would I know, having had no experience
with elegant young men in my muddled
childhood filled with raucous American
boys who lived on my street, chewed gum
and spit in the gutter.

But when my eyes locked
with Michael's and he placed an extra
cube of sugar in my tea with his bare
hand, without consulting me first,
I knew in my bones that someday
we'd be married.
Things didn't work out that way
but in retrospect it sure did come close.

NOT YET NOT EVER

One two button
your shoe doors
are shutting or pried
open then slammed
shut so air thrusts
like arrows in the
clotted atmosphere
when she's not here
he lingers needlessly
scalded scared to
face demons alone
finds it much more
convenient to dislike
his captor content
to grasp exasperation
like a cloak to wrap
up in than gather
his old playthings
into a container the
car's boot not booted
out not his idea
not hers not bloody
likely just leave just
try it try leaving one
two button your shoe.

WIND CHANGE

(child, changing)

It's not the wind on the prairie
or the wind sweeping across
the vacant pastures, shattering
glass in the barn windows.

It's the tender voice of one
small person singing a plaint,
re-playing his discordant days,
this separateness, his need

to be alone and known,
naming himself anew,
recognized as someone
brave, scared and real.

We who hover outside,
shifting against the gale,
wrap blankets about
our cold shoulders,

bending through silence
to hear hummed lyrics
strummed by the wind,
our changeable off-spring,

for are they not co-mingled,
the boy and the wind, the
wind and the boy, one storm
rife with lament and praise?

MANHATTAN AFTERNOON

In April, the nice man with the nice smile
looked straight at her and said, Desire.
It's a matter of having no desire.
He said, This must be the most delicious
pastrami sandwich I've ever eaten.
Come here and see these drawings.
This looks like the house I used to own.
Two dry gin martinis, up, with a twist.
What the hell, let's share the panna cotta.
Those new earrings are just right
on you. Also, I forgot to say I've met
another woman. It's only forty blocks
back to the hotel and such a lovely day,
let's walk and window shop. There's still
some time before you catch your train.
It's not about you, you're a nice person.
It's about desire for you. I haven't any.

CHAIR AS STAND-IN
FOR EMBRACING

move that chair
over quickly re-
arrange furniture
do not place one
chair facing the
other that way
place these arm-
chairs one along-
side the other so
both look in the
same direction
the flat bland ·
wall opposite
arms akimbo
stark arms not
reaching out
one to the other
static bent in-
ward ever aloof
ever facing away
chair as stand-
in for embracing.

SECOND HAND

I want you like a stolen vehicle
Shattered headlight, treads intact
Bucket seats of leather splendor
Weren't you once a Cadillac?

Man comes by with stolen vehicle
Rings my bell, it's strictly cash
You ride slick, your shocks absorbent
Fender-bender, not a crash.

I'll change your plates, your registration
Keep you in the shed out back
Polish up your chrome hood ornament
Babe, you're still a Cadillac.

AND DON'T FORGET
THE COURVOISIER

(a love poem of departure)

I'll really miss your liquor shelf.
I'd wander in and help myself
To vodka, gin, a glass of wine
Just sitting out there all the time
To add with lemon or some lime.

Also the Irish, Scotch or Rye.
It's very hard to say goodbye
To such a varied, vast array
I could indulge in every day.
A lesser man might start to cry.

When I am sitting home alone,
I miss your grand cru Côte de Rhone.
Or Dahlwinnie in my bed at night,
Which tucks me in when I am tight
And makes my errors seem all right.

I drink it neat and skip the ice.
A companion in my bed is nice
But nicer still is a dry rosé
Which doesn't have a lot to say
At the conclusion of the day.

Most certainly I'll miss the most
The clink of crystal as we toast
Each other with martinis dry

At five o'clock before I fly
Off in the dusk. The long Goodbye.

If we must say Farewell, Alas!
When this dire parting comes to pass,
We shall not linger. Make it quicker.
I'll miss your kiss, but Oh my love,
So much more I'll miss your liquor.

LOST AND FOUND

(in memory, John Logan)

What about lost?
I'll tell you about lost.
You wouldn't want
to try to keep track.

Losing his mother was easy.
He did it in his sleep
when he was only hours old.
A small gold locket, unlost,
sleeps curled among his socks,
one of her auburn curls twisted inside.
He didn't lose directions
to her grave, though it took
twenty years to arrive there.

Teeth, like all kids, he lost,
and his brother's love
when he beat the drums
in the high school band
instead of tackling halfbacks.
Later he lost his virtue,
then his faith, casting aside
Jesus Christ and Paradise,
the whole tidy package.
When his wife took off
with the nine kids for Red Oak,
Iowa, she left an aging swain
whose once slim form
was lost in bulges over his belt.

Drunk, another night he squandered France,
leaving his passport in the One-Eyed Cat.
And a briefcase full of notes on that lost soul,
Hart Crane, left in a parking lot in Honolulu.

His voice, reading his poems aloud,
was lavish and sad, like something
shimmering in tidal pools at dusk
or a bell ringing in a deserted church.
We, his acolytes, crowded the Community Center
to listen, never lost track of a single syllable,
each new line a kind of seduction.

In a fierce squall, he nearly lost his life
when he shattered his Chevy
into a spruce by the zoo.
Abandoning the car to the lions,
he dripped blood all over the
snow-scarred streets of Buffalo.

Days later, friends found him slumped
on his couch, a bottle of whiskey at hand.
And they drank to his luck and his love,
certain he'd break his neck for them.
Probably would.
Certain they'd find themselves again,
losing their hearts to him.

REVISITING THE OLD MAN
OF MUNNSVILLE

(in memory, Hayden Carruth)

It wasn't that long ago he sat ranting
at his kitchen table, declaiming against
injustice and pomposity, as though
perpetrators were pounding on his farmhouse door,
breaking and entering, trying to award him medals
he'd gleefully disparage. Once, in Manhattan,
he tossed a major medal, ribbons and all, right in
the stylish urinal. So much for public recognition.

Blessed be his righteous indignation.
Blessed be his brusque refusal when
invited places he'd be required to wear a tie
or neaten up his Old Testament gray beard.
He knew what was what. Get me outa here.

But how he'd cherish every living creature:
woodpeckers foraging all winter at his feeder;
the mottled cat stalking imperiously across
his kitchen counter, among unwashed coffee
cups, tubs of butter; best of all, the multitude
of unknown poets he wrote letters to,
encouraging and making kind suggestions.

Blessed be the old man of Munnsville,
attached by tubes to oxygen, trembling
equally with wrath and compassion.
"*He made sadness dazzle*" whispered his widow.
Scatter him, scatter his ashes out beside
the broken tractor, there in the fields of praise.

WE ARE LIKE THIEVES

(in memory, Clare Silverman)

Sometimes we are amazed that we expected
anything else. That deep crease in the pillow,
rumpled sheets where she so recently slept,
still astonish us. She is not coming back.
And the several sets of silver candlesticks
perch restlessly on the inlaid cabinets,
wicks taut for the match that does not
set them ablaze. Even the porcelain owl
and the ivory Chinese gentlemen seem poised
for her late arrival.

We take our time sorting strands of pearls
hidden amid her nylons, their rough luster
clasped in our living hands.
Is this the real thing?
We are like thieves among my sister's things,
invaders of her underwear, gross fingers
handling forbidden silks. No consolation
looking out at the expensive view.
Her bedside table discloses
masses of salves and potions. Too much
of this. Too much. We are unwell.
Take what we can stuff in our pockets.
These varicolored pills may help us sleep.

TRUE THINGS

(in memory, Anthony Ostroff)

Make up the miracles of your life
for me, the true things,
the narrow escapes.
You thought you could out-fox
the experts, telling outlandish stories
like a pro: your Russian father
spared from execution, crawling
through mud and slime
all the way to Detroit and your birth.
You, a boy, lost in a cave for days,
clinging to the ledge of shale.
Later, you, the dashing army sentry,
skiing down mountains to warn
companions of impending danger.
Violin, bulldozer, white-water rafting.
What else could you learn?

I thought your heart was as large
as all of Oregon: coastline,
forests, streams and cities
spilling their place-names
all over your kitchen table.

And damned if you didn't almost do it,
trick Death out of this bighearted boy.
But down you went one April afternoon
at the top of the dunes, a crash of branches,
limbs tearing at the heart of the hill,
ripping the air on the expanse
of sand and scrub and rocks.
You might as well be chopped
for kindling, loaded on a truck
and hauled home.

It was you all along,
the miracles
and all the shenanigans.
I bought the whole package.
What did I know?

TAKE TWO

Well, I'll get over it, you say
Your parents die in a desperate way
Well, I'll get over it, you say
Your children grow and move away
Well, I'll get over it, you say
Your marriage crumbles into clay
Well, I'll get over it, you say
Your cheerfulness begins to fray
Well, I'll get over it, you say
Your medicines are on display
Well, I'll get over it, you say
Your pale hair is turning gray
Well, I'll get over it, you say
A man no longer comes to play
Well, I'll get over it, you say
Sometimes it helps a bit to pray
Well, I'll get over it, you say
Insomnia is here to stay
Well, I'll get over it, you say
As age increases every May
Well, I'll get over it, you say
And so you will. One final day
You leave for good and that's okay.

ALTHOUGH YOU'VE NEVER ASKED

Although you've never asked,
I know you want to hear
about my house,
how its slim gilded birds
trace their migratory way
across the ceiling
if you chance to glance up,
how the elaborate, spindled
staircase cascades
and ascends and bends
at the landing where
library steps climb skyward,
how the rondels of stained glass
in the sun room fit snugly
in the casement windows, leaded
like some storied castle keep,
how the floors are strewn with
paper, I mean to say,
there are papers waist-deep
on the carpets and counters,
in corridors and cul-de-sacs,
papers stacked on the piano
and the adjacent settee.
This is a house composed
of paper and stucco and oak,
a house held together by
sloping doors and hope,
by climbing vines and desire
adorning the supporting walls.
This is the very house in which
I loved you in all its

meaningless constructions
and permutations,
its leaky roof and add-ons.
It's too late to improve
and out of the question to move.
This is where I live
and where I'll die.
And I could tell you more,
if only you'd ask.

KITCHEN WISDOM

Anyone's grandson, who happens to be
yours, lanky and seventeen, glances up
from his second bowl of cereal, asks:
Grandee, do you ever think about being dead?

Sure, you reply, putting away dishes.
Maybe seven or eight times every day.

Are you scared? he wonders, his long hair
drooping over his eyes while he slouches,
trying to sound curious and nonchalant
at the same time.

Scared? No, not scared, exactly.
It's hard to be scared about Dead.
I mean, it's a big blank Nothing,
like a black cavern in the sky.

Dying, on the other hand, doesn't
sound like a piece of cake.
I mean dying takes a lot out of you.

Oh yeah, he grins, catching your tone,
both serious and playful while facing
such magnitude.

Mostly, you add, I'll miss the world.
Ah, the world!
I'll miss watching you kids grow up.
What happens to each of you.

Oh, don't worry, he shrugs,
crossing the kitchen
to offer a casual hug.
You've done a good job.
We'll turn out fine.
He's probably right.

WOMAN AS GARAGE

out back out-
building out-
law leaning
outlandishly
cluttered lean-
to unattached
storage space
broken boats
lost oarlocks
hulls in rubble
mattress stacked
cracked glass
lanterns ancient
albums tattered
flattened tires
tired rims
bent inward
abandoned
babybuggies
settled in on
breezeways

you could rest
up here
you could set
yourself down
prop up
your feet
you could hang
out here
calm down here

dump trash
in baskets
shoot for baskets
shoot the breeze
blast rats or
music mad like
a banshee she
won't mind
she's open-minded
woman as garage.

THE DOWN ELEVATOR

Descending on the passenger elevator
I was going down
              going down
in the new-to-me up-
scale apartment-complex
              complex
I was close to
              moving into
when a fellow resident old-timer
              accosted me
If you are carrying
              boxes
you must not use the
              passenger elevator
you must use the
              freight elevator
if you're carrying boxes
But, I responded,
              these boxes
are empty   they are
              empty
See, there is nothing
              in them
they are empty I am
taking them
              down
to the trash
Unfamiliar with the
              ins-and-
              outs
of the massive rule-book

in my miniscule
new home
already I had
broken the law
having lived all
my previous
existence
in a place a house where
I made the rules and
there weren't any

Is this the way
things will end up
forlorn I pondered
carting
forbidden boxes
empty
in the wrong elevator of my life.

LAST RITES

Many people designate their choice of resting place,
their final space in which to linger for eternity:
the cemetery downtown where their ancestors are
silently disappearing into urban sprawl or that
expansive graveyard by a lake where headstones
take elaborate shapes like angels, pagodas, obelisks,
small temples you can peer through to see
a marble youth at rest on a catafalque.
Other types desire their ashes to be scattered
on a certain hillside or buried in the tulip patch
out back or cast in some familiar river
they swam in just last week.
It's comforting, somehow,
to know where you're going,
to rot or blow away in future days.

As for me, I'd prefer to visit The Metropolitan
Museum just one more time. I've told the kids
to take small packets of me in their pockets,
shake or sift a bit of bone and dust surreptitiously
behind a statue of a kneeling Medieval saint
or beneath a bench in the Temple of Dendur.
I'd actually prefer to reside beside a Rembrandt
or a Fra Angelico or even a Van Gogh but
I don't want the kids to get arrested for desecrating
a public place. I guess it's best to suggest they
secrete me in a pot, maybe from Mesopotamia,
that the guards won't check and I can stay there
indefinitely, avoiding the maintenance crew
inclined to sweep me into the dumpster
heading off to Riker's Island. In any case,
I'll leave sufficient cash so they can make a day of it,
stop later at the cafeteria for a tuna melt on their way out.

DIVVY IT UP

(instructions to my children)

Later grab my jewelry
hang it out the window
for all I care
twisters dangling
in the wind

watch which ones
catch the light
you'll be surprised
every time
it's not all fake

you know
the good stuff's in
the top drawer
or the bank
can't keep it straight

if the key doesn't
fit have another
one made
so what?
pry open the box

uncover baubles
rings pins necklaces
sprawled amidst
family gems and
motley acquisitions

your father bless
his lousy soul gave
me adornments
galore guilt or gilt
what to do now?

divvy it all up
where I'm going
I'll sparkle nude

wrapped in radiance
I'll ascend gleaming
look out for me
that tiny point
of light lounging

in Cassiopeia's chair
if you can't
spot me with
the naked eye
borrow Nat's

telescope blink
off and on in
the dark then
try again
I'll be there.

THE GREAT BETRAYAL
AT THE DINNER PARTY

Part way through the cocktail hour (dry martinis and twice-roasted almonds), my mother's gilded best friend Ellen -- seductively attractive to me, the little girl lurking beside the brown tufted armchair in my blue velvet party dress, long blond braids half way down my back, French braids made by my tender mother every morning before breakfast, adding tidy ribbons on the ends -- beckoned to me to follow her upstairs.

And so I did, of course, mostly out of courtesy, partly out of curiosity. She seldom paid me any personal attention, this elegant Ellen who was my mother's best friend.

I have an idea, she whispered. *Let's surprise your parents and cut off your braids. You'd look wonderful without those silly braids. Much more grown up.* I liked my braids. I really did. But what did I know? Maybe I'd look prettier with shorter hair. Ellen assured me I would.

She searched my mother's bureau and discovered scissors large enough for the job. Then, taking apart my plaits, she began to cut -- and once cutting began, there was no turning back. I was ashamed and scared. What would my mother say? My coarse hair hung above shoulder length now, sticking out at odd angles, no shape whatsoever

Ten minutes later, down the stairs the two of us traipsed, Ellen triumphant (*Look what we have here!)* and I mortified. I knew together we'd done something dreadful. I quickly burst out: *It's not my fault.* Nor was it, though my mother Peggy gasped and fled the living room to check on the simmering lamb stew. My father, bless his sociable heart, poured everyone another round of dry martinis, observed my hair would certainly grow back.

Of course it never did. I never looked remotely the same, never again felt nine, long blond braids down my back, nine my favorite age so far.

Years later, in trying to figure out why my mother's friend would do such a thing to our family, it occurs to me that her only daughter was different from Ellen. She was gawky and plain. Perhaps it came down to simple envy. *Watch what I can do to Peggy's girl.*

ONLY NOW I RECOGNIZE MY FATHER

How generous was he not to have mocked at my suitors.
How perfectly balanced, benevolent, opening doors,
How easily he offered a beer to the latest pretender,
Some slovenly lout whom I casually touched on the arm.
He would laugh at his jokes and ask him the name
        of his father
And say that he'd met him or anyway wished
        that he might,
And make me believe I was wise in my choice
        of companion
When, now I consider, how could he be less than aghast
That I in my ardor was squandering all my devotion
From moment to moment on someone outrageously borin
Who would surely be fondling my breasts way
        before midnight
In a broken-down car, parked, with the radio blaring.
And he knew in a week or a month this lackluster suitor
Would have filled up his gas tank, jauntily calling: So lon
Leaving me at the time in my father's intelligent gaze.
How fortunate was I that all my mistakes were my own.

CLEAN SHEETS DAY

My mother is the mangle
in the basement.
My mother is at angle
with the silent metal
mangle in the basement.
Her anger at the mangle
is displacement
she rants at sopping
bed-sheets and sobs
among the cases
just in case my father
listens while the old
machine keeps chugging
cellar-weeping
where it's wringing
out another load of laundry
and sweet melodies
Swing Low I hear her
singing in the basement
while my slim and grieving
mother folds the sheets.

PORCH WATCH

(for Linda)

Still here still clear
a sort of silvery
sheen on the surface
of the shimmering bucket
water filled to the brim
fresh water staying fresh
in the old tin bucket
placed on the porch just
by the back door
to warm itself in
intermittent sunlight
breaking through weeks
of overcast gloom into
another blink of afternoon.

This glowing water
could assuage your thirst
if lifted to your lips
but left undisturbed
it rests in gleaming time
who knows what time
a small nudge would
mark its spilling
so far so good
not splashed on the wood
whole weeks days months
moonlight winds storms
dark stars and the bucket
of water endures

on the back porch
no questions asked

rests in repose
while nobody knows
when it will disappear
no longer be here
but the surface is clear
a mystery a gift
this water of life
stays on into bright Fall.

NOTHING NOW ASTONISHES

not the halt
between footsteps
the slow opening
of doors
the closing

not the noisy
everyday life
in the streets
the clutter and
crash of trash

cans or shrill
voices at dusk
no, nothing now
astonishes
not even

the silent
rattle of the heart.

THRENODY

Into whose womb was she woven?
Out of whose womb did she plunge?
Is this grief that accompanies her
From one town to another?

Not long after the other hid scissors in her bed,
Not long after he chose silence,
Not long after the tall place was cut down,
Not long after all crooning ceased,
She thought she too might be unrecognizable.

Thank God her own hands reached out to her.
Thank God they were as homely as ever.
Stroking, holding herself.
Her dear old consoling attached hands.

ACKNOWLEDGEMENTS

Four Buffalo Poets: "Moving Furniture," "And Don't Forget the Courvoisier," "Woman As Garage," "Kitchen Wisdom," "Clean Sheets Day," "Last Rites."

Mezzo Cammin: "Take Two," "Wind Change."

The Quarterly: "Threnody," "True Things."

Third Wednesday: "Only Now I Recognize."

Earth's Daughters: "Nothing Now Astonishes."

Foundlings Press: "The Down Elevator."

Antigonish Review: "We Are Like Thieves."

New Ohio Review: "Manhattan Afternoon."

Woven Tale Press: "Although You've Never Asked."

The cover image comes from Whiting Tennis, "Life Guard Tower," relief with found wood, 2002.